Robin Goodfellow

Marxism in a nutshell

From the criticism of capitalism to a classless society

Table of Contents

Foreword

Since the failure of the major proletarian struggles of the 1920s, the longest counterrevolution in history has helped to confuse the basis of revolutionary theory, even for its militants. In its Stalinist, Social-Democratic, and Leftist representations, as well as in the reports made by representatives of the bourgeoisie, Marxism is disfigured. It bears no resemblance to the powerful critique of bourgeois society, to the scientific theory that since the middle of the 1840s explains the genesis, the development, and the death of this society and announces the end of class society.

During the crisis that shook the capitalist economy between 2008 and 2010, some members of the international bourgeois press decided to tip their hats to Marx. Instead of saluting him as the revolutionary who was able to make the connection between crisis and capitalism's need to overcome it, they simply acknowledged him as a "visionary" who foresaw its future failings. It is because we place ourselves in the viewpoint of the proletariat that we defend its historic programme; that we urge it to form a distinct political party in opposition to all the other parties and take the political power in order to establish a society free of social classes and the State, wage-labour, money, and mercantile categories; that we defend the revolutionary scope of this theory without and against all official and academic approval.

This short work summarizes the essence of the communist critique of political economy and is meant to offer all those seeking a radical critique of current society a condensed version of the coherence and power of the revolutionary theory. It is also meant to show that, far from being an ideal or just a wishful thinking or a utopia, the communist future is necessarily embedded in the development of the bourgeois society reliant on the exploitation of the productive class: the proletariat.

Socialism has become a science, and should be studied as such. The only school in which it can be truly understood, transmitted, and developed is the proletarian party in the historic sense of the term. The authors of this text are fully committed to this tradition, and do not recognize any validity in the critiques of the Marxism such as the "modernizations" made by bourgeois or reformist scholars, economists, and university professors. They address to a fighting class that knows by instinct what exploitation means and is seeking sound theoretic means that will help it better fight tomorrow's battles.

We have attempted here the difficult task of "vulgarizing" a complex scientific theory. Revolutionary socialism is scientific in the sense that it explains reality and militant in that it passionately defends the need of the revolution. "Vulgarization" obviously runs the risk of limiting complex demonstrations by oversimplifying certain concepts and phenomena.

Readers who wish to explore certain aspects presented in this book in more detail can refer to our more theoretical works, which are available on our website in several languages at www.robingoodfellow.info, and of course by returning to the original source texts. Nowadays, a number of websites ease the access to these kinds of source texts (although not always to the best translations).

To make for smoother reading, we have tried to keep our quotation of Marx and Engels to a minimum besides a few instances where we felt it would be impossible to improve upon the clarity of the original formulations.

Marxism is a science, and therefore a living theory whose concepts thoroughly resist to the complexity of the contemporary world (while on the contrary bourgeois political economy, not to mention its philosophy and sociology, are always increasingly idiotic). This does not hinder the fact that today it is necessary to make a considerable effort to take the theory even further, to refine the concepts and precisely apply them to the phenomena of the current capitalist mode of production, while strictly staying within the general, programmatic, framework defined by the theory. As Lenin said, without revolutionary theory there can be no revolutionary movement, and nothing could be truer today.

São Paulo - Paris - July 2013

The historical development of the capitalist mode of production

The unprecedented development of the capitalist economy and the attenuation of crises during the thirty years which followed in the Occident the end of the Second World War, the collapse of the false "communisms" in the East, the rise and development of new capitalist countries on all continents, and, last but not least, the interminable counter-revolution which, from the 1920s onwards, reduced the influence of revolutionary communism to a shadow of its former self, made it easy to believe that the capitalist system was here to stay.

Rulers, economists, journalists, and other representatives of the bourgeoisie are sure of one thing: nothing can be accomplished outside of capitalism. The economy (presumed as capitalist) seems to have become second nature to us; it seems impossible to even imagine that a society could work, live, reproduce, and develop without the categories of money, the market, exchange, and wage labour; that we could live using products of labour which are not commodities.

All of these categories, however, whose scientific Marxist definitions we will go over in the next chapter, are not eternal; they have not always existed, and Marxism shows that they have become obstacles to the development of society. In order to develop, capitalism has had to fundamentally transform relations of production between individuals, along with the modalities of production (the mode of production), to create the conditions for its own development. This process has been far from peaceful and idyllic.

The existence conditions for the capitalist mode of production.

Marx ridicules bourgeois economists and the morality tale they have spun to explain the origins of the fortunes upon which merchant's capital was first built. These fortunes were allegedly the fruit of carefully accumulated savings on the part of generations of honest, hardworking entrepreneurs, while the hedonists and the incompetent found themselves penniless and forced to sell their arms. This is obviously not really how history produced the two main conditions for capitalist exploitation: on one side the existence of a mass of workers with neither hearth nor home, the proletariat, on the other a capitalist class that monopolises the money and the means of production and subsistence, allowing the latter to employ the former. Contrary to the bourgeois economists' fable, these conditions were set up and developed through expropriation, State intervention, and a bloody legislation to discipline and hold back the emerging proletariat; through plunder, theft, pillaging, murder and other violence, not to mention the slave trade, forced labour, public debt, fiscal exaction, trade wars, and protectionism.

The development of the proletariat.

The capitalist economic structure emerged from the dissolution of feudal society. It required free workers able to dispose their own being, and therefore emancipate themselves from both servitude and the power of the guilds.

The creation of the proletariat is therefore the amassing of free individuals at one pole of the society. What is meant by "free" here is the freedom to sell one's labour-capacity to those who withhold the capital. It is necessary to have a class who possess nothing but their "own labour in a potential state" and who is faced with the necessary means to the existence of its labour: tools, raw materials, and workplaces. Unlike artisans, who both own the tools and

8

perform the labour, proletarians realize nothing because they found themselves, in a sense, naked before capital. This is a radical separation from the means of production, something that become further entrenched throughout the existence of the capitalist mode of production.

Under feudalism in England, for example, a portion of the land was said to be communal, belonging to the people, or villagers, rather than to the lords. The villagers were free to graze their livestock or farm portions of this communal land but had no claim to ownership (this was not, in other words, a form of private property). In the 17th century, the so-called enclosure movement (the fencing off communal lands) was encouraged by the State through Parliamentary acts. This allowed for the expropriation of a portion of the peasantry, who then became available to sell itself to capital.

In the chapter of the Capital, Volume I, which deals with colonization (settler colonies) – *The Modern Theory of Colonization* -, Marx uses this particular method of capitalist expansion to show that it is not the means of production themselves that create capital, but rather the fact that they exist in the face of a massive, dispossessed proletariat. In other words, capital alone cannot produce surplus-value because its production also requires a mass of completely dispossessed proletarians to be readily available to it. While bourgeois economists invent an idyllic past to explain the birth of modern society, Marx looks to the places which clearly show capitalist relations being established: settler colonies, where the producer still owns the means of production and the land, a phenomenon that had been wiped out in England several centuries earlier. This is where Marx says we can see the "secret of the political economy," in that without the expropriation of workers, capitalist relations cannot exist.

In Europe, it was through expropriation, the submission of the masses to the discipline of manufacture work, the Poor Laws in the 17th and 18th centuries, the punishment of vagrants, and other coercive methods that the proletarian masses necessary to the capitalist mode of production were created and subordinated. The history of their expropriation and the way they were groomed for their imprisonment in the manufactures is written in fire and blood. But the expropriation of the vast majority of the rural population is only radicalized with the more highly developed capitalist mode of production following the industrial revolution, as the complete separation of agriculture from domestic production such as spinning and weaving.

The genesis of the capitalist class.

In order to develop the capitalist mode of production, money and commodities had to be transformed into capital. In other words, there has to be money and the means of production and subsistence on one side, and a class of free workers on the other. The existence of this latter, however, does not automatically create a capitalist class, whose origins are varied. The oldest form is the capitalist farmer, which emerged progressively, over time. Then, as a result of the agricultural revolution of the late 15th and the early 16th centuries, a domestic market for industrial products emerged, promoting the existence of a capitalist class in that sector. This class rose in part from guild masters, artisans and even wage-labourers who became capitalist entrepreneurs, but mostly thanks to the legacy of a capital inherited from the Middle Ages, which before the capitalist era had the rank of capital: the merchant's capital and the usurer's capital. These capitalists had accumulated enough money susceptible to be transformed into industrial capital, that is to say, to buy the means of production and employ a free labour-power.

The expressions of the modern capitalism were developed from these "antediluvian forms". Before that, merchant's capital mostly played a role on the development of exchanges, in that it specializes the social function of the exchange. In other words, instead of an apple farmer selling his apples at the market and then buying shoes from a shoemaker (here we have not a barter, but rather a monetary exchange), the holder of the merchant's capital now played an intermediary role between the different producers. One of the later developments of the capitalist mode of production will be the centralization, by the merchant's capital, of the means of production in central locations, favouring to increase labour productivity. So, before socializing labour, capital first socialized exchanges.

From its inception, the running of the capitalist economy would have been neither possible nor explainable without the relation between these two opposing classes, one of which, the capitalist class, could only impose its dominance over the other, the proletariat, through exploitation.

We will now briefly explore how the historical movement of the capitalist mode of production developed from this early impulse.

The great moments of the capitalist development.

Capital has deployed throughout history by constantly deepening on what made its appearance: the valorization of capital through the purchase of labour-power that produces more value than it costs. In Chapter 2 we will explore in more detail how Marx's scientific work gave the keys to explain the extortion of surplus-value.

During its development, capital does not change its nature. In fact, it gets better at accomplishing its goal: the production of maximum surplus-value. Thereby, the bourgeoisie amasses and expands the means of production and develops the productive power of labour. One of the consequences of this is the socialization of the means of production and products of labour. What is more, the modern capitalist mode of production opens the way for the unlimited development of the productivity of labour. This development comes into contradiction with capitalism's short-sighted goals, with the quest for maximum surplus-value, and calls instead for a society for which the groundwork is already laid. A society in which there is no longer any exploitation of wage-labour.

According to Marx, this movement went through three phases beginning in the mid-14th century: simple cooperation, manufacture, and large-scale industry.

Since its beginning, capitalist production has always required the exploitation of a significant number of workers under the command of a single instance of capital, which must have reached a certain amount to advance wages and means of production.

This arrangement ensures that the collective labour-power contributing to the production process will have a level of productivity that meets the social average and, thanks to economies of scale, reduces the cost of the means of production (such as buildings). The creation of a collective worker, the result of labour-power's cooperation, allows the expansion of fields of work that can be done under the sponsorship of capital, such as major public works, for example, and brings with it an improvement in social productivity. This simple cooperation, which implies large-scale production, can be seen throughout the history of capitalist production, though it is also characteristic of a certain infancy of it with the professional manufacture[1] and large-scale agriculture.

With the advent of the actual manufacturing age, which lasted from around the mid-16th century to the last third of the 18th century, a form of cooperation based on a new division of labour emerged. As we have seen, the agricultural revolution of the late 15th and early 16th centuries led to the rise of the manufacturing production, but it is only when manufacture is the dominant form of the capitalist mode of production that the true capitalist era begins. Without detailing the numerous forms of manufacture, let us emphasize the specificity of the division of labour during this manufacturing period: here the collective worker is composed by a large number of fragmented workers. At the same time, we note a differentiation and specialization of the instruments of labour. Despite the trend to the fragmentation of tasks, the creation of a hierarchy between qualified workers and assistants, the reduction of the cost of apprenticeship, and the mutilation of workers through intense specialization, handicraft remained the basis of manufacture and the pivot for proletarian resistance. As manufacturing developed, this narrow technical basis came into conflict with production needs; to overcome them, machines were given birth.

Machinery, the industrial revolution, and the development of productivity.

In the section of Capital, Volume I dealing with large-scale industry, Marx includes a chapter on *"The development of machinery."* He begins the chapter by reiterating a basic tenet of revolutionary communism: any increase in the productive power of labour also means increased exploitation of proletarian labour-power and a refinement of this exploitation. As a result, developing

---

[1] Manufacture bringing together one or more workshops but without modifying them through the division of labour. This manufacture is at the origin of the manufacture specific to the manufacturing age.

the application of machinery under capitalism is simply a particular method of producing relative surplus-value.

Apologists of technological progress must call in again: it is directly oriented against the proletariat. It is synonymous with developing relative surplus-value, with an increased exploitation of labour-power, and with a higher valorization of capital thanks to increased surplus-value.[2]

Socialism takes back the term *industrial revolution* to mean the moment (during the early period of large-scale industry in 18th century Europe after passing through manufacture) when "mechanical production" took over manual production where tools remain central. Tools which had once been handled by man' hands now became parts in a working machine. Workers formerly made use of the tool; now the machine makes use of them. Tool-based manual production, even in a reorganized production process such as in manufacture, could only produce a limited increase in labour productivity. Machines open the perspective of an unlimited labour productivity.

The industrial revolution does not translate to the creation of machines which are an extension of the hand, but to the elimination of man from the productive process. This phenomenon opened up new extraordinary perspectives to the development of the productivity of labour. Not only does it mean that the number of simultaneous active tools can be multiplied, it also means an increase in the speed of execution. Gradually machinery seized all branches of production, "which are connected together by being separate phases of a process." Progress in one branch means progress in others, for example large-scale spinning and weaving sphere requires progress in the chemical industry so that dyes might

---

[2] For a definition of this term, see the section *Absolute surplus-value and relative surplus-value*.

14

be produced, and so on. The capitalist mode of production therefore helps to unify all human activity and put in place a "system of general social metabolism" (Marx). By weaving together the industrial fabric, interconnecting all branches of production, and considerably increasing labour productivity, capital creates the conditions for a society where collective, socialized production will allow for individual free development.

But the logic inherent to technological development cannot only be viewed from an inside perspective of the machine, neither as a movement detached from the social form in which it exists. Spurred on by the movement of the valorization of capital, the movement that integrates techniques generates fundamental social consequences for the evolution of humanity, beginning with the unification of the productive class, the proletariat.

This is why socialism calls industrial revolution the machinery phenomenon. It is not only a technological evolution, a new invention of the human history. Its arrival sets down the material basis for communism by allowing for an unlimited development of productivity and a permanent reduction in necessary labour-time, settling the basis of an affluent society. But that is not all! Machinery also induces a labour process *specific* to the capitalist mode of production and permanently creates the associated social labour. It creates the class of the associated producers who has to supersede the dictatorship of capital in order to realize the machinery potential and bring the productive power of labour to another, higher, level.

Therefore, the industrial revolution, in its very concept, potentially induces the perspective of a classless society, the communist society. With the industrial revolution, the bourgeoisie set in motion productive forces that come into conflict with the exclusive and limited end-goal of capitalist production: the production of maximum surplus-value. This conflict between the

15

trend of the unlimited development of the productive forces and the relations of production specific to the capitalism mode of production results in general crises of overproduction (catastrophic crises in that, for social reasons, society is devastated in the same way as natural catastrophes). Such crises are periodic reminders that a new society is arrived, and, with their tendency to be ever larger, they will lead to the violent overthrow of capital.

All through history, human development has been contradictorily occurred throughout class societies, conflicts, and various contradictions. Throughout this development, the question of social *productivity* has remained central. As long as human species dedicates a large part of their time to insure necessary subsistence, there is no room for socialism, even that, under the form of millenarian movements and religious utopias, the idea of an egalitarian society find its origins far back in history. The capitalist mode of production is the first in history where productivity develops on a social basis in that it allows foreseeing the satisfaction of social needs that goes far beyond just the reproduction of the species.

Some fundamental notions of Marxist theory

The definition of commodity

A *commodity* is any material object or service produced for the purposes of being exchanged. Commodities have not always existed: North America Indian tribes had never known about commodities until the arrival of European colonists. These tribes instead produced and consumed products collectively. Between the first appearance of commodities and what we know today, many societies have been developed only partly mercantile, and only in certain activities, like for example during the Middle Ages when villagers were able to continue living on their own products. Only in the capitalist mode of production is where the reign of commodities is generalized.

Nowadays, all of the things we use in our day-to-day lives are commodities, whether it is tangible objects like food, clothing, furniture, or services like public transport and certain leisure. Also, commodities are not limited to individual consumption; machines, raw materials, workplaces, work tools and, specially, the labour-power of the wage-labourers are commodities. It is the way of consuming that differs. Marx uses the term *productive consumption* to refer to the commodities consumed during the production process.

Use-value and exchange-value.

All commodities have a use to those who buy them (we can discuss about the social value of certain objects or gadgets but that is not the issue for the moment). We call this their useful value, or more precisely their *use-value*. The use-value of an object, of a commodity, is what makes it useful to me and what makes me want

17

to possess it. Up to this point, the concept is easy for anyone to grasp. Now it remains to ask why objects as diverse in their uses as a kilo of apples, a DVD, a litre of gasoline, a monkey wrench, a digital-controlled machine, a tonne of copper, a computer screen, an hour of cell-phone credit, and a t-shirt are all called *commodities*. It remains also to understand why, with $50, I can buy either one microwave oven, ten dozen oysters, fifty kilos of nails, two hammers, ten reams of paper, one pair of shoes, six movie tickets, three hours of cleaning services, etc.

The answer lies in the fact that these objects (services) have another dimension besides their use-value which we call *exchange value*. All commodities have a dual character: they have both a use-value and an exchange-value. The latter is due to the fact that they are not produced primarily to satisfy society's needs, but to be sold on the market. In a communist society, just as in the first human societies, objects produced will always have a social use and no longer have an exchange-value. It would therefore be a commodity-free society.

But what about different quantities of various objects which have the same value and can therefore be exchanged?

The answer is that two commodities can have the same value because they contain the same amount of an invisible substance in their concrete form: the human labour that has been necessary for their production.

Therefore, it is not a matter of a tailor's concrete labour making a coat, a farmer growing apples, or a papermaker producing paper, but rather the human labour in general. The labour-time spent to produce a commodity is what determines the amount of the value, of the exchange-value. Commodities are exchanged among them because they represent equal amounts of the same *general labour*, an abstraction emerged from their concrete forms. Concrete

18

labour, producer of use-values, is opposed to general labour, abstract, producer of exchange-values.

The labour contained in commodities, however, must be carried out in average social conditions of production, which obviously varies both historically and geographically according to the evolution of societies. When we say that the labour-time is the measure of the value contained in commodities, we are referring to the *average socially necessary labour-time.* Indeed, it is not because a handyman person who enjoys woodworking makes his[3] own furniture that this furniture may be sold on the market at a value corresponding to the labour-time that he actually spent in its production. The value of a table is calculated on the basis of the average socially necessary labour-time to make a new instance of the table, even though our handyman has spent far more private labour-time to produce his product. If the value of a table with similar quality of use is sold in a store by $200, for example, the equivalent of three hours of social labour, and that our handyman has spent nine hours to produce his table (including the purchase of equipment), he cannot expect to sell it for more than $200 (and definitely not by $600, the amount that represents its spending of socially valorized labour).

The dual character of the commodity is not easy to grasp. The commodity does not indicate at first sight that its value is in proportion to the amount of human labour socially necessary to produce it. Furthermore, this dual character appears as something natural. The exchange-value, which is attached to it and that conceals particular social relations, presents itself like a natural property. We will see later the importance of the mystificator character of the commodity.

---

[3] We will use "he or his", instead of the "politically correct" 20th century he/she or his/her formulas, concerning "Man", as a reference to humans, and not to "man" as a reference to males.

Labour-power.

Why do we say labour-power and not simply labour?

When workers make something, they may assemble a number of raw materials or objects, but they do not have a box or bucket stamped with "labour" next to them containing a substance which would be the "labour" that they would inject into the production. Labour is not a material, it does not exist outside of the power that is able to create it, that is to say the human ability, intellectual and physical, that one uses to accomplish a task, whether it is picking apples, assembling auto parts, or calculating the structures of a bridge.

One commodity in bourgeois society has a unique use-value: the ability to produce more value than it takes to reproduce itself. This commodity is the labour-power: the specific human ability to use intellectual and physical capacity to accomplish a large variety of productive tasks and, in the end, transform nature.

So, what the capitalist is really buying from the proletariat is not their labour, but rather this particular commodity, its *labour-power*, labour-capacity, in order to be consumed, inasmuch as its use-value is its ability to produce an additional value, an extra value, a surplus-value. No other commodity consumed during the production process give up to the product more than its own value, neither raw materials nor machines.

In order for this exchange relation to exist, there must be reached a historical relation that puts capitalists, which have the monopoly of the money and the means of production and subsistence, on one side and proletarians[4], which have been

---

[4] In ancient Rome, the proletarians (proles) were those whose only wealth was their lineage.

dispossessed of all means of production and possessing no source of wealth besides its own labour-power, which have been forced to exchange for wages, on the other. This has not always been the case, historically, such as in ancient Indian tribes and in Gallic society, and still is not for direct producers like peasants, artisans, and so on.

So how do we define the value of labour-power?

The same way we calculate the value of any other commodity: by the average socially necessary labour-time required to reproduce it. Before they are able to perform productive labour, individuals must be raised, educated, and trained. They also require food, housing, clothing, electricity, transportation... The sum of all these needs makes up the total amount of what is needed to spend to maintain this labour-power. Naturally these needs vary from place to place and times. The portion of leisure or of abundant consumption may vary, downward or upward.

There are numerous historical examples of the way the eating habits of the masses were changed to lower the cost of their upkeep, such as promoting the introduction of potatoes, or making English workers drinking tea instead of milk.

What is needed to be remembered here is that labour-power is a commodity. Like all commodities, it has a use-value (the ability to produce commodities and be the source of value and surplus-value) and an exchange-value determined by the amount of average socially necessary labour-time required to produce it.

Surplus-value.

Why do we say that labour-power, or labour-capacity, is a commodity that can produce more value than it costs to its owner, the capitalist, to buy?

Because the capitalist can exploit the labour-power for more labour-time than the average socially necessary labour-time required to reproduce it. And since the value of a commodity is nothing else than the labour-time required for its production, the value of labour-power is, in fact, lower than the value created during a working day or month. The capitalist pays for the former and appropriates the latter. The difference between the two is what we call *surplus-value*. It corresponds to the unpaid labour provided by the worker, or *surplus-labour*.

For example, if a capitalist can buy a working day from a proletarian for 100 units of currency, he has the right to require the worker to provide seven, eight, ten or more hours of labour, according to the labour-laws in place.

Let us suppose that the elements we listed above, as necessary for the reproduction of labour-power, represent the equivalent of two hours of production, that, in other words, after two hours of production the capitalist would have recuperated his advance. So what happens after those two hours? Does the capitalist then say to the proletarian: "Thank you, you have done your work well, so you may now rest"? Of course not! Instead, the capitalist will take advantage of their contract to employ the worker for the six remaining hours in a normal, legal, working day in, for example, a 44 hour work-week in Brazil (closer to 40 hours in fact, at most companies), or 35 hours in France, or more in the U.K. and the U.S.

And what exactly do these six hours mean to the capitalist? They are pure bonus, unpaid labour, free labour, and therefore what we have defined as surplus-labour, the time during which surplus-value is produced.

This is why the fights for the reduction of the working day are an essential element in the balance of power between the proletariat and the capitalist class, because they concern the time which can be spent in the production of surplus-value.

This results in an important consequence: even respectful capitalists who treat their workers "well," keeping the length of the working day within the legal limits, paying the labour-power correctly, and maintaining a good relationship with their employees, even these capitalists, despite their virtues, are exploiters due to the fact that they make their workers produce free labour, that they have not paid for.

The strength of Marxism is that it is not a morals that limits itself to denouncing the poor conditions inflicted on the proletariat, but it is a theory whose demonstration has the power of a scientific truth: exploitation is inherent to capitalist social relations. So whether bosses are "crooks" or not, they must all be eliminated, not as individuals but as the representatives of a social relation rooted in exploitation. Their time is over. According to Marx and Engels, as the productivity of labour increases, the entire bourgeoisie becomes strictly *useless*.

Wages

We have seen that labour-power, like all commodities, has a value determined by the average socially necessary labour-time required to reproduce it. And like any other commodity, labour-power also has a *price* that represents the concrete monetary expression of its value.

The value of a commodity is socially determined by the amount of labour it contains, but its market price is a function of supply and demand. Commodities are sold at a price above their value if demand is high and below their value if it is low. It is all about *variations* around a value, which is determined by the average socially necessary labour-time required to produce commodities. Yet, just to mention, this is all more complicated than it first appears. Indeed, in the capitalist mode of production the market prices of commodities do not gravitate around the value, but around prices of production. The price of production is the price resulting from the equalization of rates of profit between large masses of capital, but these prices of production are themselves ruled by the movement of the value. During crises, while lacks a solvent demand for all commodities, there tends to be a generalized fall in prices, a general depreciation of commodities; this is one of the forms of the devaluation that seizes capital during crises of overproduction.

This is also true of the labour-power commodity. What the proletarian trades as wage-labour is the price of his labour-power. We have seen that the value of labour-power is determined by the amount of time it takes to both produce and reproduce it. A longer period of education and a higher level of qualification, for example, but also a faster wearing of labour-power due to a longer working day or an increase in the intensity of the labour, all tend to increase the value of labour-power. On the other hand, there is also the influence of supply and demand regarding the variation of prices around this average value. If there are few workers of a certain qualification available when demand is high, their labour-power will tend to be sold above its value, that is to say at a higher price; but conversely, if there are too many workers, in a period of unemployment, for example, wages will tend to fall and their labour-power will be sold by a price below its value.

Despite the unemployment due to crises, Marx shows that capital maintains an "industrial reserve army" a surplus population whose role is to constantly drive wages down.

In the quest for maximum surplus-value, the capitalist class seeks to lower the price of labour-power below its value as well as to lower this value itself. In the 19th century, for example, British capitalists praised the frugality of the French worker for being underfed and therefore underpriced. They themselves by introducing cheaper food into the diet aimed at the reduction of the value of labour-power. Marx wrote: "Nowadays these aspirations were largely exceeded, thanks to the cosmopolitan concurrence into which the development of the capitalist production has thrown all workers of the globe. It is no longer question of simply reduce the English wages to the Continental Europe ones, but to lower the European level to the Chinese one in a more or less near future".

The elements that make up capital

The above mentioned concepts: labour-power, surplus-value, and wages, are fundamental to the critique of political economy, but in order to fully understand why and how capital is historically condemned we must look at its movement and the contradictions which appear there in its entirety.

Capitalists advance more than just wages. To exploit labour-power and to extract a maximum of surplus-value, they must also have available the means of production: machines, raw materials, energy sources, buildings and floors, and land in the case of agriculture. These make up what Marx calls *constant capital*. It is called *constant* because these elements transfer their value to the product during the production process. Whereas the part advanced to pay wages is called *variable capital* because it gives back a variable value beyond its initial value. This part of capital can only render a higher value, however, because it is exchanged for labour-power, the only commodity able to produce more value that it costs.

So, a commodity production which goes out each day from a factory will be made up by:

- a fraction of the value of the machines and what is more generally referred to as *fixed capital* (the fixed part of constant

25

capital); this value is not transferred all at once, but little by little, and is what economists call value of amortization;

- the value of the raw materials, fluids, etc. that go into the product; this is what is called the *circulating* part of *constant capital*;
- the value of the wages paid to proletarians corresponding to the *variable capital*; this is the part of the working day that is paid for, which Marx calls *necessary labour*.
- and, finally the *surplus-value* produced during the working day by these same proletarians, which corresponds to the part of the working day that is *surplus-labour*.

The value of a commodity therefore boils down to the amount of labour it contains, that is to say the amount of labour-time necessary to produce it bringing together all stages of its production. The raw materials that will be transformed are themselves products of labour, and therefore have in turn an exchange value in the capitalist mode of production. This value (as well as the spent fraction of the fixed capital) is added to the value that is created during the production of the new commodity. Marx says that the value of this constant capital is *transferred* to the product.

This clearly shows one of the challenges capitalism will have to face, which we will address in the next section when we look at the role of machinery. To make labour more productive, capitalism tends to increase the portion of constant capital in the production; well, this portion does not create new value, it only transfers its existing value.

The relation between constant capital (c) and variable capital (v), as expressed in the formula c/v, represents what Marx calls the *organic composition* of capital. The fact that this organic composition increases (that is to say that the mass of constant capital grows significantly in regards to the mass of wages mobilised to put it in operation) is a contradictory element in capitalist production, whose only goal is to obtain surplus-value which itself can only be produced through living labour. We will further see the consequences this has on the rate of profit and its evolution later on.

But what are the methods capital can use to constantly push this quest for surplus-value further?

Historically, Marx distinguishes two methods: the production of absolute surplus-value and the production of relative surplus-value. These two types of surplus-value are not necessarily antagonistic. They may be combined, that is to say they can reinforce one-another. In any case, absolute surplus-value cannot exist without a sufficient level of development of the productive power of labour and relative surplus-value cannot exist without a sufficiently long working day. While constituting the basis from one another, they are distinguished by the historical evolution of their relations.

Absolute surplus-value and relative surplus-value.

Firstly, when capital began to take over production through the expropriation of traditional producers (artisans and peasants, movement that we discussed in more detail in Chapter 2), it starts by *lengthening the working day*. The labour performed in agrarian societies was certainly hard and the years of poor harvests very difficult, but despite the long hours spent in the fields, peasants still had some free time: breaks, meals, snacks, home improvements during the winter months... But there was a sort of natural rhythm that dictated the way work was organized and the period over which it was carried out.

With manufacturing labour, which developed in Europe from the 16th century onwards, this rhythm was transformed considerably, a transformation that would be intensified by the transition to large-scale industry at the end of the 18th century.

The first rise in productivity was achieved by concentrating a large amount of labour-power in one place. This increased productivity made the manufacture more competitive, but it was still simply taking again the techniques used by artisans, concentrating them and rationalising their application. The only way to further increase the portion of unpaid labour was to prolong the labour-time.

Marx calls the surplus-value that resulted from this lengthening of the working day *absolute surplus-value*. If the working day is 12 hours long, for example, and only 6 of those hours are necessary to reproduce the value of labour-power (necessary labour), it would have to lengthen the working day from 12 to 14 hours to gain an extra two hours of surplus-labour. This would mean 6 hours of necessary labour and 8 hours of surplus-labour. The amount of surplus-labour, so the surplus-value, would then have been increased by one-third without affecting the amount of necessary labour, as long as the additional wearing of labour-power remained unpaid.

During the period that predates the industrial revolution, capital had no choice but to favour this kind of surplus-value. But with the limited technical basis available in manufactures, the working day could not be prolonged excessively. Besides physical limitations, technical limitations (such as the lack of sufficient lighting to allow working at night) and cultural limitations played a role as well, with social rhythms and customs contributing resistance to this movement.

It wasn't until machinery that capital was able to generalize other methods for increasing the production of surplus-value. Creating its specific own technical basis with the machine, capital,

28

through eliminating the hand from the production process based on large-scale industry, yields the means to increase the quantity of surplus-value produced while reducing the value of labour-power through developing productivity.

This is what Marx calls *relative* surplus-value, a surplus-value no longer obtained through the lengthening of the working day but instead through the reduction of the value of labour-power or through the changing of the relation between surplus-labour and necessary labour, therefore changing the relative lengths of the two portions of the working day without prolonging it.

Necessary labour represents that which is actually *necessary* in order for labour-power to reproduce its own value; beyond this, labour-power produces surplus-value. To allow a relative increase in the portion dedicated to surplus-labour without also prolonging the labour-time, either the amount of time it takes to reproduce the value of labour-power must be reduced or the value created during this same period is increased while the value (or price) of the labour-power does not increase proportionally.

Thanks to a general increase in labour-productivity, capital can reduce the value of commodities that go into the reproduction of the value of labour-power, thereby decreasing the value of labour-power and, as a result, reducing the time necessary to reproduce it. Let us return to the example of the 12 hour working day made up of 6 hours of necessary labour and 6 hours of surplus-labour. Let us suppose that the general increase in labour-productivity reduces the duration of necessary labour to 4 hours. The time spent to produce surplus-value will be 8 hours instead of 6 as before. This would also allow capital to increase the mass of surplus-value produced by one-third, but in this case without affecting the labour-time.

Likewise, by increasing the intensity of labour, capital can increase the value created during the same amount of time. As long as the value of labour-power (or its price) remains the same or does not increase too much, surplus-value increases.

Productive and unproductive labour

Marx, like a number of classical economists, such as Adam Smith, before him, distinguishes between productive and unproductive labour. The definition of productive work within the framework of the capitalist mode of production is quite clear: productive labour is labour that produces surplus-value for capital. In other words, as we shall see, the expression "productive labour" does not mean a "labour which produces something," otherwise every handyman or amateur cook would be considered "productive," so it really means *labour that produces surplus-value*.

We can therefore clearly see the crucial nature of this question, since the issue of exploitation and the definition of class and classes struggle are its background. The proletariat, the productive class, is also the only class in the capitalist mode of production that is exploited. On the other hand, if productive labour exists, there must also exist unproductive labour, and therefore unproductive workers. By contrast, when labour is exchanged for income and not for capital, it does not produce surplus-value, it is unproductive. If a capitalist who owns a cleaning business, for example, employs ten wage-earnings to clean company offices, for example, that is considered productive labour. But if this same capitalist hires a cleaner to clean his home out of his own income (which is not here capital), he is not employing productive labour because this labour does not create surplus-value during its consumption.

So one of the main criteria that allows us to determine whether labour (and therefore a worker or a group of workers performing the labour, since individualizing the issue has little interest in itself) is productive or unproductive, is to verify whether it is exchanged for capital or for income (the case, for example, of State employees).

Labour can be exchanged for capital and from this viewpoint return a profit to the capitalist, yet still not be considered productive. This is the case of all labour that arises on the sphere of circulation (banks, commercial aspects of trade, etc.) or the incidental expenses of production (insurance and accounting, for example). So only labour that is exchanged for capital within the sphere of material production produces surplus-value and is therefore productive.

It follows from that:
1. Although all productive workers are wage-labourers, not all wage-labourer is productive. Marxism shows that, even if there is an increase in wage-labour, it is the unproductive wage-labour within it that grows the fastest and which is the material basis for the rise of the modern middle-classes, salaried middle-classes. Ancient middle-classes do not emerge from the capitalist mode of production, and they tend to diminish. On the other hand, even not being producers of surplus-value, they may be producers of value (peasants and artisans, for example).

2. Productive labour is not assimilable to the one that produces a tangible product, a concrete object.

3. Productive labour is not assimilable to the manual labour. The proletariat is not made up solely of the socio-professional category "worker" or, in other words, Marx does not conceive of a working class made up of only manual labourers. This is similar to when we confuse the notion of industrial capital with the industrial branch alone. In fact, agriculture and services can emerge from industrial capital and allow the production of surplus-value.

4. Productive labour is not assimilable to the one that produces

socially useful objects. Proletarians who produce weapons or luxury items produce surplus-value and are therefore productive. In the same way, unproductive labour is not necessarily useless labour or socially detrimental. The communist society, for example, will need social accounting whose role will be all the more important even though its relative cost would be much lower.

5. It is useless to individualize productive labour. Marx shows that the capitalist mode of production has, from early on in its existence, been characterized by the existence of a collective worker (see cooperation, manufacture, and large-scale industry) that carries out material production.

6. The salaried middle-class is not characterised by a mid-level income, as it is by bourgeois sociology. The upper echelons of the proletariat or the most qualified fractions of it may have higher incomes than many members of the middle-class. What differentiates the two is the productive or unproductive nature of their labour and not their levels of wages.

Formal subsumption and real subsumption of labour under capital

When referring to the evolution of the capitalist mode of production (among other things), Marx uses the concepts of formal subsumption and real subsumption of labour under capital. By labour we mean productive wage-labour; this labour is therefore also the way in which the proletariat is subjugated to the authority of capital.

So what do these somewhat complex terms, whose meanings are often misinterpreted, mean?

At first, capital can only invest itself in what are the already established conditions of production in the society of that time. At this point, the majority of the labour is carried out with fairly traditional tools, such as the spinning wheel, the weaving loom, and all the hand tools used in traditional trades (carpentry, masonry, woodworking, pottery, shoemaking, and so on).

One of the main roles capital plays is first to concentrate a large amount of labour-power in one place (workshop, manufacture, and later the factory), naturally resulting in a general rise in the productivity of labour (see Chapter 1 on simple cooperation) which continues to increase when a technical division of labour is put in place. This rise in the productivity of labour which enables simple cooperation and after the division of labour specific to the manufacturing period allows for an increase in the production of relative surplus-value. But once this organization of labour is instituted and since the increase in productivity of labour remains limited, the increase in surplus-labour can only be in the form of absolute surplus-value.

Overall, the technical procedures in place in this first period are not fundamentally modified. Labour processes and production procedures remain the same or very similar to those used in the pre-capitalist handicraft. This is why Marx calls it the *formal subsumption of labour under capital*. The form of labour process remains unchanged, but it is submitted from now on to the valorization process of capital. In other words, the spinners or weavers working with others in the capitalist's workshop perform the same gestures with the same tools, but their social relation to these work tools and to the product of their labour has changed. Although the labour process has been inherited from pre-capitalist forms of production, it is from this point on submitted to capital and to its only goal: producing maximum surplus-value.

With the formal subsumption of labour under capital, the scale of production increases. A large number of workers are brought under the command of capital. This formal subsumption of labour

33

under capital is therefore at the origin of the capitalist mode of production and has existed from the moment wage-labourers began to work using pre-capitalist technology. Simple co-operation, like the manufacturing period, emerge therefore from the formal subsumption of labour under capital, because although its end-goal is still the production of maximum surplus-value, the labour process is not significantly transformed.

Because of this, in the formal subsumption of labour under capital, once the level of development of the productive power of labour has been established, it is only under the form of absolute surplus-value that surplus-value can be produced. Once the new organization of labour to render it more productive has been put in place, the amount of surplus-value produced using the same techniques before capital took over production cannot be increased without resorting to practices such as the lengthening of the working day. The formal subsumption of labour under capital can therefore only produce this form of surplus-value.

Socially speaking, we are dealing here with a completely established capitalist mode of production, or in other words with the social relation that chains proletarians to the instruments of labour that appears before them and outside them as *capital*. From this perspective, the formal subsumption of labour under capital is a general form of the capitalist production process. But technically, this capital has not yet transformed the general forms of the labour process; the technology used is not yet specific, peculiar to the capitalist mode of production.

Yet this first concentration of the means of labour (both constant capital with tools and raw materials, and variable capital with proletarians) combined with the ensuing division of labour, forms the basis for a technical progress specific to the capitalist mode of production. To take the extraction movement of surplus-value a step further, it is not enough to make men work for longer, but also to make them work differently.

Marx refers to the moment when capital *really* subsumes labour, that is to say when it develops its own technology dictated by the specific goal of the capital: the production of maximum surplus-value, now no longer inherited from previous forms of production.

This is why the *real subsumption of labour under capital* is an intrinsic form specific to the capitalist mode of production, its most highly developed form. It includes the formal subsumption of labour under capital, because in its general dimension which consists of submitting a large number of workers under capital, this one remains throughout the capitalist mode of production. The formal subsumption of labour under capital has therefore a specific dimension and, on the one hand, particular to a passed historical period of the capitalist mode of production, but also a general dimension that remains throughout the history of this mode of production, which is embraced by the real subsumption framework. In a way, the real subsumption of labour under capital succeeds the formal subsumption of labour under capital while also maintaining it and putting it on a higher level. With the real subsumption of labour under capital, the production of *relative* surplus-value can soar, bringing with it an extraordinary increase in the exploitation of the proletariat.

The capitalist mode of production is acquainted with a historical movement that leads it to develop itself into an increasingly "pure" model, even if this model is never fully completed in reality. All branches of production fall under the thumb of capital, which imposes itself in opposition to the independent producer. Marx says capital is "value in process", value valorizing itself. Although this expression of philosophical nature is abstract, this movement is concretely embodied in its

35

voracious quest for surplus-value, a quest for which the capitalist mode of production sets in motion the productive forces and seeks to seize all the results of science and technical development to put them at the service of this valorization, of this quest for maximum surplus-value.

It is through the development of machinery, during the industrial revolution, that the extraordinary gains of productivity, which the capitalist mode of production puts to the service of the production of surplus-value, are made possible and which communism will put to the service of the reduction of the time and the hardship of labour to allow humans to fully enjoy their free time without worrying about the future.

The rate of surplus-value, the rate of profit, and the tendential fall in the rate of profit.

We must now go further in our examination of the general movement of capital and show how the principles on which capital is founded are the very thing that will lead to its dissolution. In short, the more capital seeks to produce surplus-value, the more it comes up against obstacles to increasing this same surplus-value.

When relating surplus-labour to necessary labour, surplus-value to variable capital, Marx refers to the *rate of surplus-value*, which is defined by the equation s/v (the mass of surplus-value produced over the variable capital advanced). It measures the extent of capital's exploitation of labour-power.

Let us say that the capitalist advances $100 of variable capital for one 8-hour working day, and that 4 hours of this labour represent necessary labour. At the end of the day, the value corresponding to the living labour performed is $200 and the capitalist therefore pockets a surplus-value of $100. We would then say that the rate of surplus-value is 100%.

But among the conditions of production, the living labour, labour-power, is not enough. It can only produce because it sets in motion dead labour in the form of the means of production (machines, raw materials...) which are called, according to Marx, constant capital (c).

If we relate our $100 of produced surplus-value to not only the $100 of variable capital (v) but to the total capital advanced, that is to say c + v, we no longer get the same result.

If the constant capital c advanced is $100, it is necessary to relate the $100 of surplus-value to 100c + 100v = 200.

The rate of surplus-value is still 100%, but the *rate of profit*, which is written as s/(c+v), that is to say the surplus-value related to the total capital advanced (c+v), is only 50% (100/200).

We see here that, by definition, the rate of profit is lower than the rate of surplus-value.

However, among the conditions of the development of the capitalist mode of production we find the development of machinery and of the productivity of labour that comes with it and which results, as we have seen, in an increase in the organic composition of capital.

Suppose our capitalist buys machines which are more expensive, but which allow for an increase in the productivity of labour and require fewer workers to run them. At the same time, all things remaining unchanged otherwise, if productivity increases, so does the amount of raw materials and intermediate products used by the same amount of labour-power. Then we will have the following situation (abstracting from the productivity feedback):

200c + 80v +80s

The rate of surplus-value (s/v) is still 100%, but the rate of profit has now fallen to 28.5%.

Marx calls this phenomenon the *tendential fall in the rate of profit*. This is the most important law of political economy.[5] It is tendential because, like all laws, its action is affected by a particular set of circumstances. In this case, this law is also subject to counteracting factors. It is therefore only present in the long-term and in particular circumstances. If there were no counteracting factors, capitalism would quickly wither away.

Among these counteracting factors, Marx highlights:

- The increase in the exploitation of the labour-power through the development of the productivity and intensity of labour;
- The depreciation of the elements of constant capital: the calculation we have applied to the value of v also applies to c. Suppose that where before it took 50 hours to build a machine, now it only takes 25. This means that the portion of c represented by this machine has had its value cut in half. In the same way, if the rise in productivity overtakes the production of raw materials and intermediate products, the value of these items decreases. Capital has therefore succeeded in increasing the *technical composition* of capital while holding up the rise of the *value composition*. This is why that to define the organic composition of capital we say that it is the value composition, insofar as it reflects the technical composition.

---

[5] For further reading on these subjects, see "Aux fondements des crises. Le marxisme de la chaire et les crises", by Robin Goodfellow.

- Relative surplus population. There exists in society an unemployed or underemployed population which carries weight to technical progress because capital may prefer to employ underpaid workers rather than invest in modernization. This is the case for luxury industries in general, and the tendency to develop luxury follows the development of capital, particularly when it comes to satisfying the needs of the upper middle-classes. Generally speaking, the development of branches which employ more than the average amount of living labour helps to counteract the tendential fall in the rate of profit.

The cycle of accumulation.

Capitalist production takes the form of the following circular circuit, or cycle:

Money (money-capital advanced by the capitalist) – *Commodity* (purchase of the means of production and the labour-power) – *Production* (production of commodities within the production process) – *Commodity* (commodities resulting from the production process ready for sale; their value is higher than the value of the commodities at the beginning of the production process because they contain surplus-value) – *Money* (realization of the value of commodities into money; at the end of the cycle, the money-capital is greater than the money-capital advanced at the beginning of the cycle because it has been increased by surplus-value).

The capitalist advances capital in the form of money, converts it into means of production and labour-power to end in producing commodities. Yet these commodities are of no use to the capitalist if they cannot be sold. In other words, the movement of the transformation of money-capital into commodity-capital is of no use without the rest of the movement: the transformation and realization of commodity-capital into money-capital augmented by the surplus-value produced.

As the terms "cycle of accumulation" and "circulation" suggest, this is a circular movement which is never-ending in principle. But it would be a mistake to overlook what is happening at the different moments of the cycle. We might compare it to the cycle of water. All of the metamorphoses of the cycle must be completed in order for the cycle to be complete, but it is not irrelevant to examine it from one of its states rather than another one. There is water, the vapour produced by evaporation, clouds, rain, and back to water, these are always the same matter (H_2O) which expresses itself in various forms.

Here it is capital which appears in different forms and passes from one form into another, from the form of money to the form of productive capital (the means of production and labour-power), to the form of commodities and then back to the form of money.

Through this movement, capital achieves its objective, its "supreme-goal:" producing maximum surplus-value. In other words, the capitalist does not want to simply recover the amount invested in production, but to recover a greater sum of money.

It is important to remember that all that lies behind these objects (money, commodities) is *capital*. Capitalists throw their capital into the production process and it metamorphoses itself, constantly changing its forms, from money-form to the form of means of production (machines, raw materials, labour-power), to the form of commodities destined for the market, back to money-form, and so on. If this cycle is regular and sustained there is no problem, but if there is a long delay between two metamorphoses, the cycle may break down. This is what happens during *crises*: if the commodities produced cannot be reconverted into money, if capital can no longer continue its cycle to be reincarnated into money and be reinvested, it remains unemployed and risks becoming devalued. This is why Marx calls these crises as *crises of overproduction*: there is too much capital, too many commodities being produced which cannot be realized. At the same time, if money-capital cannot make enough surplus-value, it will not succeed to accumulate. Lack of realization and failure to convert money-capital into the elements of productive capital (means of production and labour-power) are two aspects of the same phenomenon specific to general crises of overproduction, that is to say the economic crises specific to the most developed capitalist mode of production, the first of which dates back to 1825.

But what do capitalists do with surplus-value if they do manage to realize it? If they spend all of it, there can be no accumulation. In order to pursue capital's end-goal, the production of maximum surplus-value, surplus-value must be at least partly capitalized upon, that is to say it must be retransformed into capital that can begin a new production cycle on a larger scale. If capitalists have a given amount of money to put into the production process in the first place, we have seen that they will also need to have at their disposal means of production and labour-power. As soon as they have an additional amount of money to inject into the production process, they will also have to find additional means of production: more machines, raw materials, and labour-power.

This constitutes the basis for the movement of capital, the accumulation of capital. Marx also calls this reproduction on an increasing scale, and compares it, using the words of the bourgeois economist Sismondi, to a *spiral*.

This is how the conditions for the development of a capitalist society are created. It is not enough for there to be money, there must also exist in front of money something to be employed usefully *as capital*.

In other words, it is necessary to transform money into means of production and labour-power on the market. We have mentioned that, along with commodities, the division of labour is a *sine qua non* condition for the exchange of products on a common standard: their value as a function of the amount of labour-time spent to reproduce them. Here we find again the division of labour, but on a social scale. There must exist complementary branches of industry, so that some produce tool machines, others raw materials, others electronic parts, and so on. There must also exist a class of free workers who will, under the authority of capital, provide productive labour. In this way, the production process is also a process for the reproduction of capitalist relations of production, a production and reproduction process as well as an expansion of both. This expansion ever-increasingly disadvantages the productive class.

Bourgeois economists who came before Marx, and, to a greater extent, the Economics professors of today understand none of all this. They believe that the additional value recovered by capitalists comes from the commercial sphere, that it is because a commodity is sold more expensive than its price that they are able to pocket a surplus-value, or they imagine that the means of production themselves, such as faster machines, fertile soil, and new inventions, for example, have the ability to produce value. However, as we have seen, surplus-value is in fact created in the production sphere by productive wage-labour. It is not theft, but it is the result of the exploitation of the proletarian class.

There is another point on which Marx criticizes his adversaries: the economists. As good defenders of bourgeois law, economists always portray the relationship between the capitalist and the worker in terms of two people who have entered into a contract. But this relationship should not, however, be examined on an individual level, it should be seen as the way relations between these two classes are tied, in other words, as all capitalists against all proletarians.

The goal of the movement we call the accumulation of capital is to produce maximum surplus-value. It is an absolute necessity for capital to continually expand production from the moment this latter is based upon its valorization. This means any value invested in production is purposeless unless it renders, at the end of the productive process, a greater value made up of the advanced value and the surplus-value. Capital, according to Marx, is *value in process*, value which moves to increase constantly; it cannot be otherwise as long as we stay in the logic of the accumulation of capital.

Economic relation and relation of exploitation.

Bourgeois political economy, as well as the bourgeois labour law, considers the transaction between the worker and the capitalist to be a fair dealing between two people possessing commodities and exchanging them, which in this case is a labour capacity over a certain amount of time (labour-power), exchanged for money (wages).

But Marxism shows that under the fairness of this trade lies exploitation and that this relation of exploitation reproduces and perpetuates itself. On the one hand the process of production constantly produces and reproduces capital, and on the other the workers emerge from the process as they entered it: a personal source of social wealth deprived of their own means of realization. Their work, made into the property of the capitalists, can only be realized through this process in products that flee from their hands.

Capitalist production, which is also the capitalist's consumption of labour-power, constantly transforms the products of labour into not only commodities, but also into capital, into value that drains the creative power of labour, into means of production that dominate producers, and into means of subsistence which buy the workers themselves. The continuity or periodic repetition of the capitalist process of production alone reproduces and perpetuates its own basis, the worker in his quality of wage-labourer.

Profit and surplus-profit.

At the level of society, the productive class as a whole creates a growing mass of surplus-value which is then divided among the different fractions of the dominant class in a variety of forms. In enterprise, this surplus-value takes the form of profit.

Today the term "profit" is often used, with moral connotations, to mean a parasitical "commercial" profit, and is used to condemn the fact that someone would sell a commodity above its price of production in order to gain an advantage which would be the profit. In the scientific vocabulary of Marxism, profit as a whole cannot be equated with commercial trickery, because it is a fraction of surplus-value. All commodities are sold at their value and it is because they are, taken as a totality, sold at their value that capitalists are able to appropriate surplus-value.

This surplus-value will be split into profit and rent, separating the capitalist class from the landlord class. Within the capitalist class, the profit is divided among the capitalists according to the capital they advanced. This is called the equalization of rates of profit. Commercial capitalists therefore receive an average rate of profit equal to the general rate of profit like industrial capitalists, even if their effective contribution to the production of surplus-value is lesser. The profit itself will be divided into profit of enterprise and the interest that ends up in the finance capitalist. But that is not all, because taxes are the very basis of the State and they also constitute a portion of surplus-value (as well as social wage).

44

Let us not forget the management salaries the capitalists pay themselves and the salaries (and means of production) of unproductive classes which are also forms of surplus-value.

This is the way the surplus-value is divided within society between the different dominant classes and within the bourgeoisie itself between its different fractions, and beyond. But Marx is very insistent when stressing the single source of this mass of surplus-value that is divided afterwards between different protagonists. It is well, at first, the industrial capitalist (by which we mean any capital involved in any sphere of production and not only the capitalist of industry) who guarantees the production of surplus-value thanks to its exploitation of productive wage-labour. Contrary to the claims of the branches of petty-bourgeois critiques of capitalism, the banks and the financial institutions are not the true enemy to knock down as opposed to the "virtuous" industrial capitalist. The capitalist mode of production is not based on finance; it is based on the production and accumulation of surplus-value through the exploitation of the proletariat.

Developing theories specific to agrarian questions was also an opportunity for Marx to address the various forms of surplus-profit. Whether this surplus-profit is the result of productivity differentials, social monopolies, like land ownership, or actual monopoly prices resulting from a higher demand than supply (owing to the relative rarity of a fine wine, or because it is organised by trademarks and patents, for example), they find an illustration in the different kinds of ground rent. Marx shows how, far from being a theoretical novelty and a particular phase in the history of the development of the capitalist mode of production, average profit and surplus-profit as well as competition and monopoly hinge on the basis of the action of the law of value.

Fictitious capital

Along with the accumulation of real capital comes what Marx, like other economists before him, calls fictitious capital. This capital consists firstly of securities (shares, bonds, treasury bills, trade bills, and so on) which correspond to real capital which has been loaned out (regardless of its purpose). Because these securities can be negotiated over (on the stock market, for example, with a bank, or a factoring company for bills of trade and other bills issued by a company) they are traded on private markets governed by their own laws. These markets are the sites of intense speculation which allows acquiring portions of surplus-value.

In petty-bourgeois socialism, this sphere is at the root of all crises, and the capturing of surplus-value through speculative activities and interest payments (or dividends, in the case of shares) in compensation for loaned capital is the most accomplished form of exploitation. We have seen, however, that these are simply forms of surplus-value, just like profit, rent, taxes, and the salaries of the unproductive classes. Once surplus-value is extracted within the productive sphere, it is the subject of competition and balance of power games which determine how it will be divided. Communism's goal is to abolish wage-labour and other mercantile categories rather than controlling the more obvious manifestations of social parasitism.

Another meaning (2nd meaning) of the term fictitious capital concerns the fraudulent use of borrowed capital. Once the money has been loaned, the borrower squanders it and does not use it as capital. Besides crooks and professional fraudsters, we must not forget that there is a fine line between a company in difficulty requiring credit to get through a rough patch in the hopes that business will pick up again and companies that end up mired in debt. The State itself is a major, if not the biggest, borrower in this game, zealously spending money as revenue, and may be regarded with suspicion. History is punctuated by its bankruptcies and debt restructurings, placing it as one of the biggest dispensers of fictitious capital from this viewpoint.

A final aspect of the notion of fictitious capital (3rd meaning) is found in surplus-credit. In order to realize additional surplus-value, new means of payment must be created. As soon as they exceed the needs of accumulation (there do exist other markets, so they must necessarily exceed these needs) and since, on the other hand, it is in the interest of the banks to lend as much as possible whenever they assess that their risk is limited (incompetence, greed, State guarantees, and technical feats both in financial engineering and in the automation of decision-making... these are all factors that lead to the minimization of risk, despite the fact that at one time these same factors will accentuate it), the development of credit brings with it the development of surplus-credit. This phenomenon turns into price inflation of commodities, inflation of fictitious capital (in its 1st meaning: securities), inflation of ground rent (land prices and real estate assets), and inflation of fictitious capital (in its 2nd meaning), in short, inflation of social parasitism. When inflation turns into deflation these phenomena, themselves vectors of crises, are only one of the most visible aspects of the crises of overproduction which have their origin in the very heart of capitalist production.

Capitalist Dynamics and the Social Classes

Unveiling the mystifications of capital.

In his time, Marx managed to accomplish work that was both scientific and revolutionary. It was scientific because it went beyond the various phenomena noticed by different protagonists of society to show their deeper motivations, providing an explanation that broke with the interpretations of the bourgeois economists of the time. It was revolutionary because he was able to see who provided the material conditions for revolutionary rupture behind the functioning of the capitalist economy. What's more, the scientific work could not have been accomplished if Marx had not approached these questions from a revolutionary point of view, the point of view of the proletariat and of the society of the future: the communism. This is why Marx's major works on the subject of the economy are subtitled "a critique of political economy."

More than a century and a half after its birth, the materialist concept of history is still struggling to impose itself. Put into a defensive position since the end of the 19th century, being reinvigorated by the Russian revolution, annihilated by the counter-revolution that followed the failure of the revolutionary wave of the 1920s (the defeat of the German, Hungarian, Chinese, ... revolutions, the involution and then counter-revolution in Russia with the triumph of Stalinism), Marxism still has not ended to learn lessons from the defeat of the proletariat. The systematic reexposing of the concepts, theoretical elements, and conclusions first put forward nearly a century and a half ago, along with their application to the understanding of the evolutions and mutations of the contemporary capitalist mode of production, is necessary in the movement for the emancipation of labour.

The evolution of the social classes

The evolution of the social classes, the productive class included, is one of the most important questions facing Marxist theory today.

The 20th Century will be remembered as both the liveliest and the deadliest century in history. World population quadrupled and life-expectancy rose significantly while at the same time wars claimed the lives of 120 million victims, and 800 million were affected by malnutrition while on the other extreme, 300 million were considered obese. Malnutrition of course brought with it a cortege of tragic consequences: shortened life-expectancy, high infant mortality (6 million deaths a year today), and a variety of physical and mental illnesses.

The capitalist mode of production has progressed even faster than population growth. Wage-labourers make up an ever-increasing majority of the global active population. In countries where the capitalist mode of production is the most highly developed, wage-earners make up 80 to 90% of the active population. Then, the proletariat has come to make up the majority of society. The old social classes of independent peasants, artisans, and small business owners are shrinking, and their so-called "independence" is only formal, and their existence is coiled into the pores of bourgeois society. At worst, their activity is simply the antechamber of the general precariousness and unemployment.

Agriculture, for example, which is the world's number one employer, no longer represents an absolute majority of the active population. A large mass of this agrarian population, like that of peasant farmers, for example, produces value, but no surplus-value. It does not have salary relations with capitalists, but they are linked with landlords if they do not own their own land property. In the most developed countries, it now represents a very small portion of the active populations, whereas in Marx's day it made up the majority. Within it, wage-labour plays an increasingly important role. The capitalist mode of production increasingly seizes agriculture, subjects it to its laws, and ruins the peasantry, who is forced to join the industrial reserve army and swell the urban populations.

Besides the proletariat, the capitalist mode of production has two other basic social classes, the capitalist class and the landowner class. The analysis of price formation in agriculture and in the production of raw materials shows that the least fertile lands (whether for mining or resource extraction) in the worst locations are used as the basis for setting the production prices around which gravitate market prices. In the capitalist mode of production the relative prices of raw materials and basic resources essential for life are higher than those of other commodities because industrial luxuries are easier to produce than agricultural necessities. Moreover, the monopoly of land property makes this process even harder by slowing down the development of productivity in these spheres of production. Beyond these phenomena, we must also consider the effects of monopoly prices in the narrow sense, like those held by producers of the world's finest wines, for example.

Taking into account these different phenomena allows us to see how harmful the capitalist mode of production is to the social metabolism.

The contradictions inherent to the capitalist mode of production push the antagonism between town and country, the imbalance between the urban and the rural, to their ultimate limits. This contradiction reaches such heights[6] that the bourgeoisie, failing to attain a harmonious distribution of the population over

---

[6] From now on, more than half of the world's population has become urban (up from 5% in 1920), and the vast majority of this number is piled up in major urban centres.

50

the territory, is forced to take responsibility for this latter and to feed and maintain under perfusion the populations it excludes from its system of production. Therefore, the masses of people expelled from agricultural lands end up crowded into the outskirts of the megalopolis.

At the same time, urban rent has skyrocketed. In France, for example, it has far surpassed the ground rent in mass for a long time. Even though buildings (whether residential or for productive tasks) take up much less space than agricultural lands, their overall prices are much higher, and the relationship between the price per square metre of the most opulent housings or offices and the worst agricultural lands continues to grow. This ratio has now reached a million to one in France. Indeed, in the most fashionable Paris districts the price per square metre easily reaches on the average €10,000, while the worst agricultural lands are sold at around €1,000 per hectare. If we consider the most extreme examples, this already considerable gap increases tenfold.

Bourgeois society will never succeed in properly feeding humanity, nor will it ever be able to provide decent housing, nor manage territories, forests, the soil, the health and well-being of the populations, and the metabolism between man and nature, in a way that benefits the mankind as a whole.

Old and new middle classes

What is true of agriculture is also true of industry and service sector; the stranglehold of wage-labour stretches out and makes the dominance of capitalist production always more evident. Besides the peasantry, the artisan sector, and the still powerful commercial sector which make up the classic, historical middle classes, a new, modern, salaried middle class has developed. As we have seen, the capitalist mode of production devalues commodities in its quest for maximum surplus-value by reducing the average socially necessary labour-time needed for their production. But this growing mass must be sold, and capital must double its efforts and its unproductive spending on market research, advertising, sales forces, credit, insurance, and the like in order to circulate commodities and realize commodity-capital into money-capital. Circulation-time increases relatively over production-time. The increasing number of sources of capitalist accumulation along with their hordes of small businesses leads to the creation of a class of small capitalists whose wages and income come under surplus-value and require a maintenance cost proportional to their numbers. At the same time we see the development and maintenance of intermediary categories, in both large and small companies, whose role is administration, accounting, and business management.

And finally, modern capitalist societies have seen considerable development of the State and the bureaucracy. As they are paid with State funds, that is to say through taxation and borrowing, State employees are neither exploited (that is to say they produce no surplus-value and do not face capital in the sale of their labour-power), nor are they proletarian. Their labour-power is not exchanged for capital, but rather for income. With the defeat of the proletariat in the 1920s and the subsequent rejuvenation of capital (particularly after the Second World War), there followed several decades where the growth of production of surplus-value coincides with an increasing qualification of labour-power. This was only achieved by mimicking the communist program through the realization of a social democracy, by bringing progress in terms of working hours, health, and education within the limits of the capitalist mode of production, all the while maintaining the iron fist (the police, the army, etc.) and the State bureaucracy. All of these phenomena brought about the creation of State employees and made the State a major, if not the biggest, employer.

All these phenomena indicate that wage-labour does not *sensu stricto* imply a relation of exploitation. When labour-power is exchanged for income, or when it is employed in the circulation

52

sphere, or also constitutes one of the incidental expenses of capitalist production (accounting, billing, administration, for example) it is unproductive; it produces neither value not surplus-value, although it may still render a profit. All proletarians are by definition wage-labourers because the only thing they possess is the sale of their labour-power, but not all wage-labourers are proletarians.

The considerable expansion of the productivity of labour since the Second World War can be explained in two ways.

- The first is that this social wealth is produced by the *totality* of the wage-earning population. And yet, in the developed world, this population receives an equivalent that varies between half and two-thirds of the GDP. Then it is easy to conclude that both the absolute and the relative exploitation of the proletariat (which in this case is taken together with the general wage-earning population) will not worsen, and that the interests of capital and labour are therefore compatible.
- The second is to maintain Marx's crucial distinction between the productive and unproductive portions of the employed population, the latter of which may be wage-earners themselves. In this case, it is necessary to bring back the production of surplus-value to the sole productive portion. This means that the value and surplus-value are produced by the proletariat alone and not by the totality of the wage-earnings. As a result, it is clear that the exploitation of the proletariat is much greater than the first explanation allows and it is shown that the interests of labour are irreconcilable with those of capital.

The consequence of this last point in determining the possibility of communism is crucial; in fact, the concentration of the productive sphere on the proletariat, and not on wage-earnings as a whole, shows the unprecedented productivity attained through the development of the capitalist mode of production, productivity whose product *must* be wasted to avoid the pot boiling over. This shows the amazing capacities of a reorganization of productive functions; the elimination of a number of unproductive sectors, even socially harmful, and the generalizing of productive labour throughout the society as a whole while decreasing individual labour-hours, would bring about considerable changes from the very first phases of a revolutionary process.

At a time when, faced with the catastrophic perspectives offered by the bourgeois society, many currents favour "degrowth," a Malthusian limitation of wealth production, often in the name of ecology and the protection of the planet, it is important to recall that the origin of the economic catastrophes that ravage society is social, and that a society led by the revolutionary proletariat is an absolute necessity.

The role of the modern middle classes.

A large part of this category of unproductive wage-earners makes up what we call the modern "middle classes." The wage-labour is what distinguishes them from old middle classes made up of artisans, peasants and the like, as we discussed earlier. Contrary to what bourgeois commentators claim, this phenomenon of the expansion of the salaried middle classes was perfectly predicted by Marx. Living off of surplus-value, and therefore off of the exploitation of the proletariat, these classes defend interests "close to those of the exploiting classes" (Marx).

In Capital, Volume I, Marx sets out the role of capitalist managers by defining its social function, psychology, and evolution. Capitalist managers (to be distinguished from the owners of capital) personify capital, "functioning as personified capital." Their function is to make them produce maximum surplus-value,

54

which involves both obtaining the best yield possible from labour-power at one time as well as increasing the accumulation of capital, both in width and in depth. Production for production's sake and the glorification of the development of the power of productivity of labour, these are the functions of the capitalist, a fanatical accumulation agent.

Capitalists are only interested in exchange-value, which is why frugality, austerity, and greed are quite rightly the most prominent characteristics of the pioneers of capitalist development. But these bourgeois "virtues" have weakened, over time. Capitalists have succumbed to the mermaids of unproductive consumption of surplus-value. It is true that the progress of the concentration and centralization of capital has led to an increasing production of surplus-value with which capitalists can increase its consumption without significantly affecting its accumulation. What is more, this consumption has become a professional necessity, since the flaunting of wealth is a way for capitalists to obtain credit, inspire confidence, and maintain the sphere of their relationships. But this tendency meets its limits among capitalists, since enjoyment and spending are done with a sort of guilty conscience because of their propensity to the contrary which is necessary to stoke the fires of accumulation.

If capitalists give up enjoying accumulation in order to accumulate enjoyment, they are also giving up their social function. For capitalists, the eventual sanction of consuming surplus-value unproductively instead of accumulating is to be beaten out by the competition.

From the perspective of capital as a whole, two opposing pitfalls lie in wait for the capitalist mode of production. If we imagine a society made up of only proletarians facing a capital whose only goal was the production and accumulation of surplus-value, it would result in a spike in the development of the productive powers and of the productivity of labour. Such prodigious development would then quickly undermine the bases for this same capitalist production, pushing the devaluation of capital to the extreme while at the same time creating a massive accumulation of commodities which would grow increasingly difficult to sell or, in other words, to realize. This would mean capital driving into overproduction and crises that much faster. On the other hand, the development of production for production's sake, partnered with a development of the capitalist's personal wealth, could lead capitalist production to wither and lose its momentum, to purr before its amassed profit without seeking to systematically push the productive power of labour. This would mean that capital would leave behind its historical mission that much sooner.

Since 1845, Marx and Engels insisted that the very productive powers that the capitalist mode of production develops also become destructive powers. While the capitalist embodies the passion of accumulation, the love of production for production's sake, it is necessary that the passion of spending and of consumption for consumption's sake be expressed in society as well. We have seen that the capitalist cannot have completely this function without renouncing its being. This is why production's dialectical counterpart, consumption, must be expressed by another class. And so a class which represents spending, consumption for consumption's sake, must develop. Since the capitalist class, despite developing its penchants for consumption, cannot carry out this function alone, and since this function contradicts its social function at a certain point, the class which best represents spending and consumption is the middle class.

Such is the economic function of the middle class, according to Marx. It embodies the passion of spending and thus plays a regulatory role within the capitalist mode of production. The volcano of production is limited in its expansion while at the same time being stimulated. But beyond this facet, the middle classes also play a political and social role as a shield for the dominant classes.

The capitalist class and landed property

Capital concentrates itself, in that it is accumulated in the same centres, through the development of capitalist production. Under the drive of the progression of productivity; of the development of the minimum amount of capital necessary to make productivity meet its social average; of the effects of competition and crises; and of the development of credit which allows some individuals to access social capital, capital centralizes itself, or, in other words, all things considered, that the number of centres of accumulation is reduced. For example, it is said that there are 80,000 multinational corporations, a dramatic rise, which produce 10% of the global GDP and control two-thirds of world trade. What is more, their subsidiaries are said to produce more than the volume of world trade. Social forms of property (joint-stock companies, public enterprises, cooperatives, pension funds, holdings, and so on) are developed in parallel to the credit system, as well as the separation of capital and property is maintained while their respective protagonists become professionals: on the one hand capitalist managers who assure capital management, on the other hand finance capitalists who claim the capital's property interests. The line between capitalists and landowners becomes blurred and these classes tend to merge, with some buying the lands, forests, and buildings that are then subject to corporate property firms while the rest become shareholders and capitalists. As an owner class, the bourgeoisie is increasingly remote from the production process that it continues to hinder while facilitating crises. This is also how it reasserts its parasitic nature.

The concentration and centralization of capital

The concentration and centralization of capital are phenomena which are relative and non- absolute. Just like the influence of multinational capital and of the biggest enterprises continue to grow relatively, small and even the smallest businesses are also proliferating. The accumulation of capital in new centres, whether through detachments to older societies or through supplies of new capital, is even greater especially since these new sites of accumulation do not require large amounts of capital to exist. The development of services that imply closer relations between individuals and relative physical proximity tend to fall under this frame. Marx describes an identical phenomenon when talking about the production of luxury items, which employs a larger workforce: the production of more refined, higher quality or luxury products increases as the development of productivity increases. The development of qualified labour-power which can gain autonomy more easily because the design process takes up an ever-increasing portion of the total labour-hours required to produce commodities also contributes to the success of this movement.

The reasons these small businesses develop recurrently are many. Where the desire to escape wage-labour may motivate some, the majority may have no choice but to try to exist by themselves on the marketplace because they cannot find wage-paying employment. On the other hand, an array of more or less archaic statutes and protections which, in most countries, apply to occupations like pharmacist, notary, physician, lawyer, architect, and so on, slow the expansion of wage-labour in these sectors. These smallest enterprises are also essential in that their existence allows the most productive enterprises to create surplus profit and serves as a regulator to them under all forms. Last but not least, *innovation* is often synonymous with the small enterprise, which is more agile than its big enterprises counterparts. A Darwinian selection process for new products, services, and markets develops.

58

A hundred may try, but only ten will emerge, and only one will succeed. This successful enterprise will then be bought out for a good price by the big enterprise.

This movement towards concentration and the continual emergence of new production units also applies to agriculture. Although world population quadrupled over the 20th century and by the end of the century almost half the active population was employed by the agricultural sector, the number of peasants and peasant-landowners also increased. This created an overwhelming disparity in productivity between large-scale capitalist agriculture and the peasantry which, due to its lack of property, could not even produce enough for its own subsistence.

Productivity, which had reached 1000 tons per active per year for a few million actives in developed agriculture, fell for about two-thirds of the active agriculture population, hundreds of millions of people who were affected by the so called "green revolution", to 50 or down to 10 tons depending on whether they have available animal traction or not. Finally, the remaining third (a few hundred million people) living in destitution produced only about one ton per year per active.[7]

This level of productivity, setting aside the methods used to attain it and its limitations, potentially menaces hundreds of millions of farmers to disappear and forces them to move to the cramped cities; dialectically, a few million people practicing rational agriculture would be enough to fulfil the agricultural needs of the mankind by freeing labour-time. More than ever the agrarian question, much like the resolution of the antagonism between town and country, are at the heart of the social revolution.

---

[7] Mazoyer, Marcel. Protecting Small Farmers and the Rural Poor in the Context of Globalization. FAO, 2001.

Accumulation and crises

The quest for maximum surplus-value leads the capitalist mode of production into crises of overproduction. These crises have a periodic nature, and their severity is tendentiously related to the degree of the capitalist development of production. The more production is developed, the more these crises tend to have more severe social consequences. Crises of overproduction are characteristic of the most highly developed capitalist mode of production. The first of these crises occurred as early as 1825, and in the nearly two centuries since then, the bourgeois world has been regularly shaken by these highly destructive social earthquakes that spread desolation. And their frequency and intensity will not decrease; in fact, they will likely repeatedly reach new record highs. These facts leave helpless and ridicule as the economists' predictions and theories as the policies, "reforms" and other attempts to regain economic control over the development of capital.

In its quest for maximum surplus-value, capital develops the productivity of labour as though it was not limited by the mode of production itself. The large mass of commodities must be realized as money and a certain relation - which capitalist production tends to violate - must exist between productive consumption and individual and collective unproductive consumption. By failing to find a large enough market for this large mass of commodities, restricting the wages of the productive classes, and stoking the fires of accumulation that upset the relation between production and consumption, bourgeois society promotes the overproduction of commodities. On the other hand, if the accumulation of capital does not create enough surplus-value, if the growth of productivity is broken down and the rate of profit plunges drastically, then it is the overproduction of capital, over-accumulation, which menaces it.

At the same time, fictitious capital (shares and the like) also swells under the combined effects of the accumulation of real capital, speculation, and surplus-credit. Credit is one of the most important factors in fostering tension of productive powers and causing overproduction.

The quest for maximum surplus-value takes several forms:
- lengthening of the working day;
- raising of the productivity.

Other forms favour the creation of more value and surplus-value simultaneously, such as:
- developing the intensity of labour, which involves creating more commodities of the same value in the same amount of time;
- developing the complexity of labour, meaning the same labour power will produce more or less value depending on the type of the labour, simple or complex, it is being used for;
- developing the quality of labour, meaning the more qualified labour power has relatively more value than a less qualified one producing more value in the same amount of time;
- optimizing the position of national labour in the international division of labour.[8]

---

[8] The international application of the law of value is fundamentally transformed in that, on world market, the most productive labour acquires a higher social value as long as competition does not force it to lower this value. This means one hour of labour in a more developed country can be exchanged for three hours of labour in a less developed country, for example. If these two countries have trade relations, the former exploits the latter. France and Brazil, for example, have comparable GDP's nowadays, but Brazil must employ an active population triple the size of France's, and therefore expend a total of three times more labour to obtain it, and this does not take into account the differences in annual labour-time and in the relative size of unproductive classes. This law is also used by multinational corporations to spread out production across the globe to best serve their interests. This also allows corporations get around State fiscal and social policies and, in doing so, put pressure on these policies.

In doing so while also continuing to pursue its ultimate goal: maximum surplus-value, capitalist production develops productive powers within the limits proper to this mode of production. Upon doing so, the potential of production, and overproduction, is increasingly important. In order to postpone this contradiction and counteract its effects, capital implements a series of responses different in nature. We can classify them according to the type of their responses:

1. Facilitating sales, the realizing of the social product = credit development.
2. Seeking out new outlets and outside areas of accumulation = exports, the fight to dominate new markets.
3. Increasing need and creating new needs = development of advertising and marketing to give commodities a new appeal.
4. Diversifying and creating new needs, creating new use-values = development of the means of luxury consumption. One of the appeals of this sector is that in general it produces a larger amount of surplus-value due to the fact that it employs relatively more living labour. These branches also have a lower organic composition than average, which favours a rise in the rate of profit.
5. Historical evolution of use-values and needs driving the unit value of commodities to a slow-down. The "revalorization" of use-values[9] and the evolution of needs = yesterday's luxuries become today's needs.
6. Planning the obsolescence of commodities. Organizing the wasting of resources.
7. Fixing capital. Accumulating fixed capital which are not productive immediately (major highway structures, public

---

[9] The automobile, for example, has not stopped evolving in terms of equipment and options. Its relative price has not so much dropped as it has remained steady, despite progresses in productivity and the substitution of certain materials (a phenomenon that might affect pricing either way).

infrastructure, canals, and so on), absorbing surplus-value without immediately affecting the productivity of labour.

8. Development of a class of consumers that consumes without producing: an unproductive class. A consumer class is a necessity. Underconsumption theorists, notably Malthus, predicted this need. This cannot be met by the proletariat, whose consumption is limited and whose relative wages fall with the development of capitalist production, which fulfils it. The raising of real wages could certainly occur, but it would necessarily be within strict limitations. This modern unproductive class is the salaried middle-class. As it develops, the rate of accumulation is limited and the demand of means of consumption rises, bringing with it the consumption of sophisticated products and luxury goods.

9. Tendential fall in the rate of profit and in the rate of accumulation. Accumulation and growth slow down, and capital postpones these contradictions by giving up its mission.

Crises do not mechanically lead to war or revolution, but they do contribute to causing them, and while revolution is the proletariat's ultimate solution for ending its own exploitation and halting the catastrophic path of the capitalist mode of production, war will be capital's ultimate solution for regenerating itself, at the risk of destroying mankind.

Towards a classless society

One of the major dramas in recent history has been the political disappearance of the proletariat, which has been stripped of its revolutionary nature. Its international party twice fell into the hands of counter-revolutionary forces (during the second and third internationals). We are not going over the details of the historical circumstances that led the proletariat into the counterrevolution in the corner of the 1920s after it completed the most heroic feat of emancipation in its history at the international scale, the high-point of which was the 1917 October Revolution in Russia. From that point forward, the proletariat all but disappeared as an independent political party and therefore as a class aware of its historical goals. Not only have its representations, traditions, songs, flags, and emblems become the symbols of its oppression, but its theory has also been sterilized, denatured, caricatured, and transformed from revolutionary theory into a social preservation mechanism. Meanwhile, societies based on the capitalist mode of production like the USSR, China, Cuba, and others have become the established references for real socialism.

Throughout all this, the proletariat has only existed as the far-left wing of democracy, being in thrall to the parties of other classes. In doing so, in the most developed countries it has merely traded its emancipation for improvements in its situation. A reduction in working hours, a higher standard of living, longer life expectancy, an education for its children, access to healthcare, and so on... in other words, all the elements of so-called "social democracy". It has also pushed for the conquest of political democracy and expanded universal suffrage and women's rights. The number of countries under democratic constitutions or organized as democratic republics continues to grow. The proletariat has therefore won the battleground for the final battle against the bourgeoisie; it has allowed the bourgeoisie to direct the development of the productive powers to the point where its contradictions are so accumulated that the evidence of the need for a classless society that can overcome them is increasingly obvious.

Although it has not quite returned to its revolutionary struggle, the world proletariat is still in a position that makes it, as the only exploited class, a revolutionary class whose goal is the communist revolution and the complete overthrow of the current society's framework. This revolution is more than ever a vital issue for all of humanity. Nothing came to deny which was already the essential purpose of the 1848 *Manifesto of the Communist Party*.

The political capacity of the proletariat will obviously depend on the circumstances and on its readiness and energy to organize itself as an independent, international political party remaining coherent in its revolutionary program and opposed to all other parties. Its historic power, however, remains unchanged because it is engraved on the heart of the social relation which characterises the capitalist mode of production. The proletariat, the productive class, not only produces surplus-value, but also produces capital. It reproduces the entirety of the capitalist social relation. But in the capitalist society, this relation appears under a reversed and mystified form.

The proletariat and its alienation.

At the heart of productive labour and the production process, the proletariat produces value through its labour, reproducing the value advanced for constant capital and wages, plus surplus-value. This value not only slips from proletarians, it is also turned against them, so that their labour is transformed into their opposite, into capital by facing them. They are dominated and confronted by their own labour. Marx calls this phenomenon alienation, meaning being estranged from oneself. Exploitation (which, let us not forget, only affects productive labour and therefore the proletariat) is at the same time alienation. The other classes are also prey to the general mystification that masks the true nature of social relations, the personification of things and thingification of the relations of production[10], the fetishism of commodities and capital, and even the fact that capital and the earth appear as independent sources of value, living entities able to produce value by themselves. Yet these classes can neither unveil these phenomena by themselves through scientific analysis, nor shatter them by overthrowing the capitalist relation.

In Chapter 1 we discussed the origins of the capitalist mode of production, and in Chapter 2 we went over Marx's analysis of commodities. The existence of commodities presupposes a society in which community ties that set down *a priori* the human activity framework as a social activity have been at least partially broken. This means the disappearance of the social relationships evidence. Each producer produces privately and has no contact with anyone unless through exchange. And yet it is *products*, attained through the producer's labour, that are being exchanged and are now not simply useful objects, but also commodities. Not only does this mean that human relations now seem mediated by the exchange of commodities, but this very exchange is now necessary if social relations between people whose activity is now separated and carried out privately are to exist at all. The fact that the

---

[10] Marx never uses the term "reification", and even less as an autonomous concept as Lukács or bourgeois philosophers will later do. He systematically qualifies the nature of the social processes that are converted into things and are dialectically confronted with their opposite: the personification of things. Indeed, on the original German text of the Capital, Marx says: "Personifizierung der Sachen und Versachlichung der Produktionsverhältnisse", or "personification of things and thingification of the relations of production" (cf. The Trinity Formula - Capital, vol. 3). We have chosen to utter the somewhat unusual term "thingification", which immediately relates to "thing", instead of "reification" to avoid either the lukacsian (or the bourgeois philosophers) a-dialectical reduction or even the petty-bourgeois logic that regrets the situation of being surrounded by too many "things".

66

socialization of labour is now carried out through exchange, through a mediation that is no longer controlled by the individuals themselves, creates a sort of veiled reality which Marx compares to a religious phenomenon.

From the moment the production of commodities is generalized and labour-power itself becomes a commodity, the mystification it brings with it increases. The more the capitalist mode of production is developed, the more this mystification is intensified. With the development of relative surplus-value and the labour process specific to capitalism, this mystification creates a complete reversal in the way social relations are conceived.

The capitalist class owns all the means of production and exchange in all their various forms. This is how capital appears as society's driving force, its productive face. Marx uses the word "reversal" because capital appears productive when it in fact produces nothing on its own. Capital simply puts all of the elements necessary for production into contact and sets them in motion. Yet these same elements (on their bases, since they historically evolve) were also used to produce in pre-capitalist forms of production: all production requires materials, means of labour (tools, for example), and an agent of production, the worker.

Capitalist social relation therefore masks, and even reverses the real relation underlying it. This is how capital appears "productive," creator of wealth, when in reality this is the role of human labour.[11] By stimulating the overall movement, continuing

---

[11] This is illustrated in the vulgar discourse of the bosses who talk about the "risk-taking" and the "responsibility" of entrepreneurs and others. The bosses tend to say that they "give the labour" when in fact it is the opposite, it is proletarians who freely give away a portion of the labour-time in which their labour power is used. When proletarians internalize this argument, they might say "who will give me labour if there are no bosses?" Engels clearly wrote: "We have seen at the very beginning that the so-called "productivity of capital" is nothing but the quality inherent in it (under present-day social

to seek maximum surplus-value, and developing the productive power of labour, capital hides the fact that the source of this surplus-value and the very thing that allows for the development of capitalist civilization is the productive labour realized by the proletariat. The proletariat not only produces the material basis for the society which it thereby helps to reproduce and expand, it also reproduces and perpetuates capital and its inherent exploitative relations. This creates a diabolic vicious spiral in which the proletariat creates a foreign being that slips from it becoming its dominator. Capital therefore confronts the proletariat not only through concrete forms such as machines and facilities, for example, but also in a more general, anonymous form that exploits and dominates it. Scientific and technological progresses turn over against the worker.

Mystification is perfected through circulation and competition. Interest-bearing capital, fictitious capital, and even the earth itself are seen as sources of revenue completely divorced from labour. The equalization of rates of profit between equal masses of capital employing unequal amounts of labour-power also obscures a process too vast to be contained by individual capital. Forms of capital such as commercial capital, that move within the sphere of circulation and participate in this equalization process, contribute to the impenetrable veiling of social relations. The randomness of the successes and failures of individual capitalists, who are subject to competition, also contributes to the mystery of capital production. Counter-revolutionary forces often successfully lean on this mystification as their basis, falling victim to their own best intentions. These forces will direct the anger of the masses towards the banks, "finance," and financial capital, for example, all the while touting the virtues of industrial capital. This tends to make people forget that the latter is at the heart of the exploitative

relations, without which it would not be capital at all) of being able to appropriate the unpaid labour of wage workers." (*The Housing Question*) relationship and effectively subjugates the proletariat, making it produce maximum surplus-value in its various forms (profits, interest, rent, taxes, and so on) which are the subject of much disputes between the different segments of the bourgeoisie and its accomplices.

Throughout this process, the very essence of human labour is reversed. This is why capitalist social relations are historically the most violent: they deny the very being of man who is subjected to capital, that is to say subjected to the value in process. As violent as the relations between master and slave or lord and serf may have been, they were still relations between persons and were clearly identified as power and exploitation relationships. After all, Spartacus knew why and against what and whom he should and would rebel.

In the capitalist mode of production, the social relation, the relation between classes take the form of a *thing*, the capital, the *value in process*, that dominates the proletarian. This is why the proletariat may feel powerless at times; capital dominates everything and seems like a *deus ex machina*, an invincible naturalised force as fixed as the sky and the mountains. And yet capital is nothing but an inversed figure of reality, and rebelling against it is simply a way of setting the world right side up. Such is the role of the revolutionary theory and revolution itself, since the weapon of criticism cannot, of course, replace criticism by weapons. The revolution of the modern proletariat differs from all those that came before it because it will not be limited to bringing to power a new class who can develop a new mode of production. Instead, it is the reunification of the human species with itself and the definitive abolition of all conditions of exploitation imposed on one class by another.

This will only be possible, however, because the capitalist mode of production, through its tendency to increase the productive
69

power of labour, has developed the objective, material conditions that lay the groundwork for a new society that does not neither need the framework of private property nor a dominant class to develop itself. Moreover, this development cannot take place without the abolition of private property, which has become an unbearable obstacle. Social classes must be abolished, not for moral reasons, but because they are obstacles to social development.

The frightening feeling of never being able to escape the domination of capital comes from the fact that the process of exploitation functions as a spiral, where all the exploited class's energy is concentrated in front of it strengthening and developing the conditions of its own exploitation. And yet, in describing this process, we are also outlining the conditions for its destruction, since the proletariat, its life-force, is also the only class that can grind it to a halt. It need only regain its autonomy and break its ties with capital to begin the revolutionary transformation of society, towards a classless society.

In *Capital, Volume I*, Marx describes communism in the following way:

"Let us finally imagine, for a change, an association of free men, working with the means of production held in common, and expending their many different forms of labour-power in full self-awareness as one single social labour power. All the characteristics of Robinson's[12] labour are repeated here, but with the difference that they are social instead of individual. All Robinson's products were exclusively the result of his own personal labour and they were therefore directly objects of utility for him personally. The total product of our imagined association is a social product. One part of this product serves as fresh means of production and

---

[12] Marx alludes to Robinson Crusoe, the character of the famous novel by Daniel Defoe.

70

remains social. But another part is consumed by the members of the association as means of subsistence. This part must therefore be divided amongst them. The way this division is made will vary with the particular kind of social organization of production and the corresponding level of social development attained by the producers. We shall assume, but only for the sake of a parallel with the production of commodities, that the share of each individual producer in the means of subsistence is determined by his labour-time. Labour-time would in that case play a double part. Its apportionment in accordance with a definite social plan maintains the correct proportion between the different functions of labour and the various needs of the associations. On the other hand, labour-time also serves as a measure of the part taken by each individual in the common labour, and of his share in the part of the total product destined for individual consumption. The social relations of the individual producers, both towards their labour and the products of their labour, are here transparent in their simplicity, in production as well as in distribution."

Behind the capitalist mode of production lies the communism.

The possibility of a classless, Stateless society where wage-labour no longer exists is not a dream that has to be made into a reality. Communism is already possible because its material foundation, starting with the socialization of the means of production, has been laid out during the development of the capitalist mode of production. As we have seen, capital, in its movement, tends to become concentrated and centralized, creating vast, planned industrial groups owned by transnational corporations across the globe, such as in the auto or aeronautic industries. This development, through the world market, results in a completely tangled economic fabric in which it is almost impossible to distinguish and abstract islands that could be protected from crises or be exempt from the laws of capitalist production.

But this tendency to exclude smaller producers, group together productive powers, and rationalise techniques at the international scale comes up against the obstacles inherent to the capitalist mode of production. Marx calls this the contradiction between the development of the productive powers and the relations of production, because these relations have become *too narrow* at a certain point in their historical development. Production itself requires large-scale, borderless coordination, which conflicts with bourgeois and national property relations. Considering the catastrophic path capital is on, it would be best if important policies on energy, natural resources, agriculture, space planning, and manufacturing production were decided and consciously managed on a global scale according to the interests of associated producers instead of being based on the demands of the production of surplus-value characteristic of capitalist production. This means capital is now confronted with an untenable contradiction. Its own interests force it to increasingly unify the productive apparatus and the organisation of commodity and money circulation, and develop the productive power of labour as though it were limitless, yet it cannot pursue this movement to its apex without negating itself.

As we have seen, this contradiction is often expressed through potentially worsening crises of overproduction. Private property and wage-labour, along with the social division of labour, have gone from being factors of the historical development of capital in its inception to actual hindrances to the future development of humanity. Like a compressed form lying within a too narrow frame, the communist basis which stays on the heart of bourgeois society only requires to come out a strong enough force to shatter this narrow frame. Private property itself takes a social nature through movements like nationalization, regionalization, municipalisation, and other forms of public capital, as well as cooperatives and anonymous societies that allow for a centralization of power and the dispersal of property through holdings, institutional investors, and pension plans. This effectively abolishes private property within the framework of private property. From a materialist point of view, this is one of the bases for the development of communism, which, far from being an unattainable ideal, is rather a necessity due to the very development of society.

A world market is another condition of the existence of capital, and in it, Marx saw one of the material conditions necessary for the development of the international communist movement he envisioned. After the revolutionary failure in Europe in 1848, Marx and Engels questioned whether the revolution might suffocate in such a "small corner of the world" while capital still had considerable expansive prospects across the rest of the globe. From his part, Stalinism was forging the doctrine of "socialism in one country" to develop capitalist relations of production in Russia and to dominate by crushing all autonomous expressions of communism internationally. Communism is in total contradiction with national development, and cannot exist if not on an international, global scale. Today the considerable development of the capitalist mode of production across the planet, despite the unequal levels of development from region to region, makes the material possibility of a transition to a classless society more than mature.

In his various writings, Marx barely describes or *explicitly* defines communism and its contents. Yet every time it is mentioned, it is presented as the radical reversal of the *status quo* and the recovery by the mankind of its vital functions, after throwing off the capitalism gangue. The communism is a society that abolishes alienating labour, the wage-labour, structuring necessary labour and free labour on another basis. Through the socialization of the means of production and exchange, it is the community of associated producers that make the decisions and organize society. The free development of each one requires the reduction in necessary labour and its distribution between all members of the society in working-age and capable to work. While developing a polytechnic training, society struggles against the social division of labour by generalizing manual labour, versatility of activities, and working hard to eliminate the antagonism between town and country.

In communism, *money and the value-form of the products of labour are eliminated.* Individuals will be assigned a portion of the social labour for a predetermined period of time (which will be much shorter than what it is now), in compensation for which they will be able to consume, once the elements necessary for the expansion of society, collective consumption, and for other members of society who are unable or no longer able to work have been deducted. This consumption will be limited, at first, but will eventually only be limited by their own satiation and common sense.

The revolution's goal is to *abolish wage-labour.* In the community of associated workers the relations of dominance between the owner of the means of production and the proletariat will no longer exist. Thanks to the mediation of the community, the work of individuals immediately becomes social.

Marx emphasizes this immediately social nature of production many times. In communism, "individual labour no longer exists in an indirect fashion but directly as a component part of total labour." (*Critique of the Gotha Programme*)

The *indirect fashion* Marx is referring to is the merchant relation that connect the capitalist class to the proletariat, relation that only exist because the former has the monopoly of the means of production and exchange and the latter has only its own labour-power. Overturning the terms of this exchange allows the true human nature of labour to express itself, and it also means that the

74

productivity of labour acquired through the development of machinery truly serves human needs and no longer be completely ruled by and for the maximum valorization of capital.

It was already true in Marx's time and is even more so today: the time is more than ripe to establish the conditions for eliminating the private property of the means of production and exchange and to enjoy a collectively organized society.

The conditions for revolutionary rupture.

This brings us back to the contradictions that naturally undermine this mode of production as a result of the very way it is socio-economically organized. By constantly pushing for higher productivity of labour and through developing the productive powers, capital is creating the conditions for a new society. It also proves by itself that the relations of production specific to the capitalist mode of production are too limited to allow for its further development. There must be established a new mode of production, new relations of production that correspond to a classless society and bring humanity out of its prehistoric era so it can consciously plan its future. Marxism shows that this is an ineluctable phenomenon, and that the history of the capitalist mode of production is "the revolt of modern productive forces against modern conditions of production." This revolt regularly erupts in the form of crises during which capital, in its various forms (machines, money, commodities, labour-power, and so on), is brutally devalued, its commodities destroyed, machines at a standstill, bankruptcies, disastrous drops in prices, unemployed labour-power, and more.

In other words, the increasing rise in the productivity of labour, thanks to the use of machinery and science in the production process, is the best guarantee that today's society will eventually and necessarily lead to an affluent society, but it is also the biggest threat to the very foundations of such a society.

There comes a time when capital and the capitalist class not only *can* be overthrown - because the material basis for collective, immediately social labour free from mercantile constraints and the valorization of capital has sufficiently been developed - but also *must* be, in order to ensure the continuity of the human history.

Yet this process will be neither gradual nor mechanic. If today's society is pregnant with a classless future society, the baby is so big that it must be immediately pulled out by forceps from the belly of a cruel mother ready to commit infanticide. There can be no "spontaneous" transition at the very moment when the productive powers attain the level at which communism can emerge in a "natural" manner. A discontinuity, a revolution is necessary in order to shatter the thousand ties of the mercantilism. The primary condition for this revolution is the conquering of political power by the proletariat organized into a distinct political party opposed to all other parties.

In the same way that capital creates the conditions for its own abolishment, it also creates a class that will carry out its sentence: the proletariat. Marx wrote that "The proletariat must be revolutionary or it will not exist at all." A proletariat can only exist as a carrier of this revolutionary power, as a conscious class organized into a political party, armed with a scientific understanding of the world through Marxism, and able to predict and enlighten a sustained action that will overthrow the power of the bourgeoisie and its society.

Marx and Engels believed that the proletariat could only exist as an organised and therefore conscious social force by constituting itself into a political party. As Engels put it in *The Housing Question*, "the views of German scientific socialism...[:] the necessity of political action by the proletariat and of its dictatorship as the transition to the abolition of classes and, with them, of the State." He goes on to say that this "had already been expressed in the *Manifesto of the Communist Party* and since then on innumerable occasions." In these other occasions, the condition of "the constitution of the proletariat into a political party" is clearly laid out.

By taking the appropriated measures to demolish the bourgeois State, abolish private property and exchange of commodities, the revolutionary proletariat will break the infernal cycle that transforms proletarian labour into its opposite while also repositioning the society's productive powers. This does not mean that communism will be able to immediately realise its entire programme, it merely means that there is a qualitative leap which can potentially take society from one sphere into another one. This is the phase of political transition that Marx and Engels called the dictatorship of the proletariat.

A revolutionary party will have to define the measures which will be necessary *today*, based on the development of modern productive powers that are much more developed than in 1848, in order to destroy the machinery of State and take society to a classless society.

These measures, which may vary from one country to another and the setup of which depends on the balance of power and the international revolutionary situation, might look something like these:

Labour:
- An immediate and drastic reduction in working hours and integration of polytechnic training within these working hours, including among other things, how to manage the proletarian semi-State whose organisation goal is ultimate simplification.

- The generalization of labour and of manual labour among all members of society who are in working-age and capable to work.
- The banning of all night work and any unnecessary shift work other than in healthcare, security …
- The creation of measures that socialize domestic labour like cooking, cleaning, laundry, childcare …
- A rotation of and division of collective tasks through civil service.

Economy:
- The development of the public sector through free access to services such as healthcare and education …
- The State-ownership of banks and insurance, creating a unique new entity.
- The setting up of social planning and accounting to allocate labour power among the major branches of industry.
- The proletarian State ownership of major corporations.
- The creation of measures that help unify small companies into larger entities, and the pooling of resources to increase social productivity, one of the conditions to reduce working hours.
- The abolishment of indirect taxes. Progressive income tax. The abolishment of inheritance. The institution of a social pass based on working hours (the equivalent of the labour-time vouchers promoted by Marxism in the 19th century) for managing individual consumption. This pass is not money, because it cannot be accumulated and cannot be used to pay a salary to labour-power.

Territory organisation:
- The requisition of housing so as to immediately remedy conditions for those living in poor housing.
- The halting of construction development in large cities and their suburbs. The creation of measures that help reconcile the

town and the country. The development of labour-power in the agriculture, forestry, and ocean industries.

Security:
- The arming of the proletariat and the creation of militias insuring the tasks of police.

Administration:
- The abolition of parliaments and the dismantling of State and local administration in order to re-establish the management of social life within the community of associated producers.
- The settlement of territorial councils (soviets) in charge of the administration of society and holding executive, legislative, and judiciary authority.
- The election of responsible representatives that may be recalled at any time.
- The representatives paid salaries equal to the average salary.
- The unification of all countries having accomplished revolution and the abolition of borders. ·

Education:
- The creation of an education which, from childhood onwards, combines the learning of fundamental skills, manual labour, sports, creativity, and collective life.

Religion:
- The total separation of church and State. The relegation of religious life strictly to the private sphere.

Conclusion

The capitalist mode of production has played a crucial role in the development of humanity. It has developed the productivity of labour and the machinery, created the world market, continuously unified production and exchange conditions, and, most importantly, created the proletariat: an international class capable of seizing the productive apparatus and leading society to a society free of exploitation and social classes. The capitalist mode of production has then created the conditions that pave the way to a superior society.

The continuity of the capitalist mode of production, its survival, its hold over all means of production and of life, and its continued mad course are full of disasters for humanity. By pursuing the development of the productivity of labour, capital continues its quest to produce maximum surplus-value and subjugates a growing number of proletarians, while the simultaneous development of its productive fields turns them onto the streets. By ruining all other forms of production, it also creates a situation in which the hundreds of millions of African, Chinese, Brazilian, and Mexican peasants, among others, along with the millions of Europeans and Americans who are unemployed and excluded, do not even have a place in this society based on the exploitation of the proletariat.

Although all the conditions needed to create a harmonious way of life for humanity exist, famine, crises, wars, and other catastrophes lie in the menu of the coming century. Only the proletariat can rise up to overthrow the *status quo* and establish the classless society: the communism.

From the same author

Crisis of capital, crisis of company (in French)
Towards the foundations of crises. Professorial-marxism and crises (in French)
The Marxism and the Democratic Republic (to be published)
Marxism and the industrial revolution
Business cycle at USA since 1929

Other texts are available on the website:
www.robingoodfellow.info

Robin Goodfellow Editions
BP 60048
92163 Antony cedex
France
ISBN : 978-2-37161-012-5
Dépôt légal : Juin 2016

9 782371 610125

http:// www.robingoodfellow.info
robin.goodfellow@robingoodfellow.info

Title: Marxism in a nutshell. From the criticism of capitalism to a classless society.
Type of document: Printed text
Author: Robin Goodfellow
Edited in: Paris
Editor: Robin Goodfellow
Edition date: June 2016
Number of pages: 83
Presentation: Front cover in color
Format: A5
ISBN: 978-2-37161-012-5
Language: English (eng)
Publisher: lulu.com
Printed in France

Front cover: Plate extracted from *The mamals of Australia* de John Gould via Wikimedia Commons.

The platypus, aka duck-billed platypus (*Ornithorhynchus anatinus*), belongs to the unique egg-laying mammal order. To Marxism, it particularly symbolises the complexity of the reality, the humility that science has to retain before the state of its knowledge (its truth is relative and provisional), and the fact that in the organic worlds there is no hard and fast lines between concepts. In brief, the platypus is an invitation to the dialectical reasoning.

Online sales: lulu.com